EMPEROR

Lord Armstrong

Ken Smith

•TYNESIDE TRAILBLAZERS•

Tyne Bridge Publishing

*Front cover: Lord Armstrong at the launch of the cruiser **Pandora** on the Tyne at Elswick in August 1889.*

Acknowledgements:

The author would like to thank Jimmy Donald, Dick Keys, and the staff of Newcastle City Library for their help and support in the research and production of this booklet.

Illustrations ©Newcastle Libraries & Information Service

Emperor of Industry: Lord Armstrong of Cragside
© Ken Smith, 2000

ISBN: 185795 165 4

Published by
City of Newcastle upon Tyne
Education & Libraries Directorate
Newcastle Libraries & Information Service
Tyne Bridge Publishing
2000

www.newcastle.gov.uk/tynebridgepublishing

British Library Cataloguing in Publication data: a catalogue record for this book is available from the British Library.

Printed by Bailes the Printer, Houghton le Spring

Contents

The Reluctant Lawyer

On August 19 1884 Sir William Armstrong waited tensely in the entrance hall of his great country home, Cragside, at Rothbury, Northumberland. Soon the sound of carriages and horses' hooves would be heard clattering along the main driveway to the house. He was about to welcome the Prince and Princess of Wales as his guests during an official visit they were paying to the North-East. The couple were to stay at Cragside for three nights.

The royal visit was a major highlight of Armstrong's long and extraordinary life. Before he stepped from the house, bare-headed, to welcome Prince Albert Edward and his wife, Princess Alexandra, some of the most important events of that life may have flashed before his mind. These might have included his invention of the hydraulic crane and the Armstrong gun, his gift of the beautiful Jesmond Dene to the people of Newcastle or perhaps his satisfaction in seeing his money put towards humane causes.

His life featured what many would regard as a contradiction – Armstrong's company produced deadly weapons of destruction, yet his charitable donations and gifts advanced the welfare of numerous people, enhancing their lives through improvements in health, education and leisure. In addition, his company, which also made peaceful products such as cranes and bridges, provided employment for thousands of people and contributed greatly to the economy of Tyneside.

William George Armstrong was born on November 26 1810

August 1884. The royal procession passes under a triumphal arch in Newcastle's famous Grey Street. The temporary arch had been specially put up for the occasion. 'Radicals' were said to have criticised the large amount of money spent on the decorations for the visit.

at No. 9 Pleasant Row, Shieldfield, Newcastle. His sister, Anne, had been born seven years previously. William was the son of a

William Armstrong at the age of 20, as depicted in a portrait by Ramsay, 1830. Encouraged to become a solicitor by his father, he nevertheless spent much of his spare time investigating mechanical and scientific matters.

prosperous corn merchant, also named William, who had migrated to the town as a young man with little money from his home village of Wreay, a few miles south of Carlisle, Cumbria.

William senior found a job in Newcastle as a clerk with a firm of corn merchants. He was evidently a man of ability and energy, for he became a partner in the firm and when the other partners retired he took over the business. William senior's interests, however, extended beyond corn, money and financial transactions. He had an inquiring mind and was intensely interested in mathematics. It is not surprising that he was a keen member of the Literary and Philosophical Society of Newcastle upon Tyne, a society formed to promote science and the advancement of knowledge.

Pleasant Row, Shieldfield, Newcastle, where William Armstrong was born.

William senior became a close friend of another leading member of the society, Armorer Donkin, a wealthy solicitor of the city. Armstrong and his family often spent holidays at Rothbury where Donkin had a country home. The lawyer had no children and he treated William junior and his sister Anne like his own children, becoming an uncle figure to them. Meanwhile, their father became a Newcastle councillor and served as mayor in 1850.

William junior suffered from ill health during his boyhood and was forced to spend long hours at home because of bouts of illness, which may have been the result of a chest problem. It was during these periods of sickness that he began making toy machines from simple materials.

He also paid visits to the workshop of a joiner where he produced woodwork and learned about the various tools of the joiner's trade. This interest in the practical world of making things was the spark which would lead him to important achievements in the world of mechanics and engineering.

William junior was sent to various schools in the Tyneside area and then at the age of 16, in 1826, to a grammar school at Bishop Auckland in County Durham. Here, his growing enthusiasm for mechanics and engineering led him to pay frequent visits to William Ramshaw's engineering works in the town. He became friends with Ramshaw and fell in love with his daughter, Margaret, who was eventually to become his wife.

Perhaps at this time William junior envisaged himself taking up a career as an engineer or scientist. But his father had other ideas. The elder William Armstrong had already mapped out his son's future. He wanted him to become a lawyer and made arrangements with his old and trusted friend Armorer Donkin for William to train with Donkin's Newcastle practice as a solicitor.

Many years later Lord Armstrong was to comment: 'The law was not, of course, of my choosing. My vocation was chosen for me, and for a good many years I stuck to the law, while all my leisure was given to mechanics. A great friend of my family's, Mr Donkin had a very prosperous attorney's business. He was childless. When I entered his office I was practically adopted by him. I was to be his heir.'

As Lord Armstrong admitted, it was an attractive prospect. A secure, well-paid profession and the promise that Donkin would leave him his fortune when he passed away. Yet it seems

William junior was a reluctant lawyer, although he dutifully bowed to his father's wishes and achieved considerable competence in the profession of solicitor.

Armorer Donkin, the wealthy Newcastle lawyer who encouraged Armstrong's ventures.

Despite this reluctance, his life seemed destined to follow the path his father had intended and, after a spell gaining extra training in London, in 1835 he became a partner in Donkin's Newcastle law firm. In the same year, he married his sweetheart Margaret Ramshaw. He could now look forward to a successful career as a solicitor.

However, he continued to pursue his passion for mechanics in his free time. He often visited the factory owned by Henry Watson in High Bridge, Newcastle, and saw telescopes, clocks and other items being made there.

Such visits showed that William Armstrong had the mind and inclination of an inventor and engineer. His talent and ability in this field would lead to his invention of an efficient hydraulic crane and to the foundation of the great Elswick Works in the West End of Newcastle.

The Hydraulic Crane

Armstrong's interests outside the office were not confined to mechanics and engineering. He was also a keen fisherman and he enjoyed the sport as a boy during trips to the River Coquet at Rothbury. It was said that he learned a great deal about angling from a Rothbury workman named Mark Aynsley, who was so skilled in the art of dressing flies that they would nearly always 'fetch' a Coquet fish.

'I was scarcely ever away from the waterside and fished from morning to night,' Armstrong recalled when he was an elderly man. 'They used to call me The Kingfisher.'

It was while on a trout fishing trip to the River Dee at Dentdale, north-west Yorkshire, in 1835, that he first became fascinated with the idea of using water power to drive machinery. As he rested by a river between casting his line, he watched an old water wheel in action which supplied power to a marble works and was struck by the fact that only a small part of the power of the water was used to drive the wheel. He thought that a much greater force could be achieved even if the energy in a small quantity of water was concentrated in one column.

It is not recorded whether Armstrong caught any trout on this occasion, but he certainly returned to Newcastle with the idea of water as a motive force swimming through his mind. He drew up plans for a rotary engine powered by water and the device was built at the High Bridge works of his friend, Henry Watson, in 1838. His twin interests, mechanics and

A drawing of Armstrong's first hydraulic crane, which operated on the Quayside, Newcastle. The crane proved a great business success. Many were supplied by the Elswick Works to docks and railways throughout Britain and abroad.

angling, had proved fruitful.

Although no businessman took up the invention, Armstrong continued to develop his water power ideas. Eventually he devised a piston engine instead of a rotary one and decided that it might be suitable for driving a water-powered (hydraulic) crane.

The inventor's interest in water continued and in 1845 he suggested a business venture. This was the setting up of a company to supply Newcastle with good quality water from the Whittle Burn, a tributary of the Tyne near Ovingham, and creating a reservoir from where supplies could be piped to households in the city. A number of leading Newcastle men backed the scheme, forming the Whittle Dene Water Company. Eventually six reservoirs were built and after a number of years the business became known as the Newcastle and Gateshead Water Company.

Also in 1845, Armstrong suggested a plan to put into practice the ideas he had developed for the hydraulic crane. Supported by his legal partners, Donkin and G.W. Stable, he approached Newcastle Corporation and asked if he might adapt a crane on the Quayside to water power by using the pressure in the water pipes in the lower part of the town.

Armstrong would demonstrate that his hydraulic crane could unload ships faster and more cheaply than existing ones. The inventor and his friends, including Donkin, offered to carry out the modification and trials of the crane at their own expense. The councillors agreed to the scheme, prompted to a large degree perhaps by the fact that the corporation would not have to pay the bill for what might prove a costly failure.

However, the adapted crane proved highly successful and three more hydraulic cranes were installed on the Quayside. These were built at Watson's High Bridge works. The efficiency of his invention led William Armstrong to consider setting up a business to manufacture his crane and other hydraulic equipment. He therefore resigned from the legal practice.

Far from opposing Armstrong's move, Armorer Donkin, the man who had given him so much support over the years, was in favour of the idea and together with three other Newcastle men, George Cruddas, Richard Lambert and Addison Potter, backed the venture with money. Armstrong also contributed his own share to the project.

In 1847 the five business partners bought five and a half acres of land at Elswick, two miles west of the centre of Newcastle, and set up a factory there. The land was situated on the north bank of the Tyne between the river and a branch line of the Newcastle and Carlisle Railway. The riverside location was to prove an important asset for the future when the company would build warships and guns.

Armstrong threw himself into developing the new business, which was named W.G. Armstrong and Company, working long hours to ensure the success of the venture. In founding the Elswick Works he was greatly helped by partner George Cruddas.

One of the first orders received for hydraulic cranes was from Liverpool Docks. Yet at one point it seemed the order would not be forthcoming. Jesse Hartley, the engineer in charge of the dockside cranes at Liverpool, was sceptical when he first heard of the hydraulic crane's advantages. He was said to have ridiculed the invention.

However, he took up a challenge to visit Newcastle and see the crane in action. When he arrived at the Quayside he met a crane driver known as 'Hydraulic Jack' – real name Jack Thorburn – who was a great champion of Armstrong's invention. Jack was skillful at performing all kinds of feats with the crane and he duly laid on an impressive demonstration of its capabilities using a hogshead of sugar unloaded from a ship.

Taking the controls, 'Hydraulic Jack' began his 'crane spectacular' by running the sugar up to the head of the jib at great speed. Then he let it descend equally rapidly. However, he gradually reduced its speed as it neared the ground and stopped it gently before it touched the quay.

This display must have impressed Jesse Hartley, but more was to come. Next, 'Hydraulic Jack' swung the load around in a wide arc, continuing to lift and lower the sugar at great speed as he did so. Hartley's doubts were ended. He returned to Liverpool and recommended adoption of the invention for the port's Albert Dock.

The Merseyside engineer's visit to Newcastle may well have been one of the factors in the early success of the Elswick Works. The story of 'Hydraulic Jack' and Jesse Hartley helped to spread the fame of William Armstrong's ingenious water-powered invention.

Other early orders received included cranes for the Edinburgh and Northern Railway and hydraulic machinery for dock gates at Grimsby. Soon, more docks and railways were turning to Elswick for their needs.

But Armstrong was not content to remain merely a builder of hydraulic machinery. He eventually branched out into the fields of armament production and shipbuilding. Guns and cruisers joined the peaceful hydraulic crane on the list of products.

The mastermind behind all these developments was a self-taught engineer. Armstrong had no formal education in his chosen field in the way that today would be considered essential. But he enjoyed a well-off background, a sound general education and the backing of men with money and influence. These factors enabled his great talents to flourish.

The Elswick Works went on to enjoy many years of success and expansion, becoming Newcastle's largest employer. By 1863, 3,800 people worked at this great industrial base on the Tyne. The company was without doubt a major contributor to the development of Tyneside as an industrial area and to its prosperity, providing much needed work for many people. Housing to accommodate the workers and their families sprang up throughout Elswick which was transformed over the years from a village to a major urban area of Newcastle's West End.

Armstrong is shown in thoughtful mood in this portrait, based on a photograph. He was said to have been capable of applying himself to the solution of problems with intense concentration.

Elswick Empire

On July 17 1876, the newly-completed Swing Bridge across the Tyne between Newcastle and Gateshead opened for the first time to let a ship pass through. The vessel was the Italian warship *Europa* which was on her way up river to the Elswick Works where she took aboard a new 100-ton gun for delivery to the Italian navy. The iron superstructure and opening machinery of the Swing Bridge had been built by Armstrong's company.

Not surprisingly, among those present to witness the event was Armstrong himself and one of his company's most important partners, Andrew Noble. Thousands of spectators lined both sides of the river and crowded the High Level Bridge to watch the Italian vessel sail through accompanied by two tugs.

However, the spectators laughed as a coal wherry (small steam barge) came into view and positioned herself in order to be the first vessel to sail through. As the bridge swung open the wherry led the way, followed by the River Tyne Commissioners' steam launch, with Newcastle's Mayor W.H. Stephenson aboard. Immediately behind them was Armstrong's steam launch *Bee*.

Then came the *Europa*, with a crew of 110. Four pilots were aboard. As she neared the bridge, the *Alexander Pirie*, a ship lying near the Guildhall on Newcastle Quayside, fired several shots in salute. An immense cheer went up from the crowds as the *Europa* then glided through the open bridge.

The gun which she had come to collect was the largest

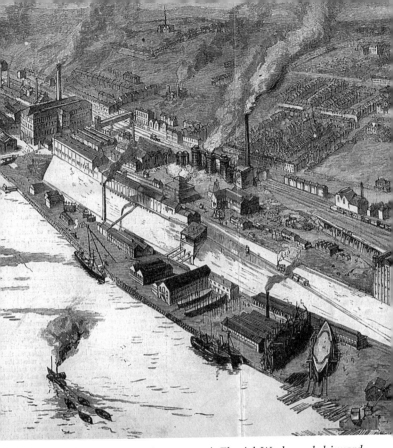

A bird's eye view of part of Armstrong's Elswick Works and shipyard on the banks of the River Tyne during the 19th century. Hydraulic cranes, guns and warships were among its products.

made by Armstrong's firm at that date and was the first of a batch of six 100-ton guns to be delivered to the Italian govern-ment. The gun was loaded on to the *Europa* at the Elswick Works jetty. The following day the ship departed the Tyne

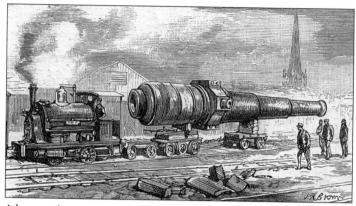

A locomotive moves a 110-ton gun at the Elswick Works. Heavy guns were supplied to foreign navies, including Japan.

bound for the La Spezia naval base in Italy where the gun would be fitted to the warship *Duilio*.

Armstrong had first turned his attention to armaments during the Crimean War of 1854-56. He had learned of the immense difficulties British troops encountered in moving two heavy muzzle-loading guns on to a hill-top position at the Battle of Inkerman in 1854. Prompted by this, he set to work with the aim of designing a field gun which was lighter, and therefore more mobile, but which also had a greater range and accuracy.

It took Armstrong only a month or so to draw up the fundamental concept. This showed that he was capable of applying himself to the solution of a problem with intense concentration and dedication. His idea was to build a breech-loading gun with a strong, rifled barrel made from wrought iron and with a steel inner lining. The gun would fire a shell rather than a ball.

He then took his proposal to the Secretary for War, the Duke of Newcastle, and the government agreed that he should build several of the guns on an experimental basis.

The first of these weapons was tested on the moors of Allenheads, Northumberland, and it was said that people living in the remote area thought that war had broken out when they heard the rumbling of gunfire. The *Newcastle Daily Chronicle* commented that 'his targets were placed upon the opposite side of a deep valley where nothing more valuable than grouse or lean sheep ran the risk of being shot'.

In 1855 the gun, a five-pounder, was ready for inspection by a government committee of armament experts. The trials were a success, although the officials clearly felt the gun and its shells were too small. In 1856 Armstrong's Elswick Works manufactured a larger test gun, an 18-pounder, and the experts were greatly impressed with its accuracy and range. In 1859 they declared the Armstrong gun superior to all its rivals.

Armstrong drew up a deed in which he surrendered his patents for the gun to the British government. He received a knighthood as his reward. The honour was bestowed upon him on February 23 1859 when he was presented to Queen Victoria.

In addition, Armstrong took up the post of Engineer of Rifled Ordnance to the War Department, later also becoming the superintendent of Woolwich Arsenal, the government's main arms factory. His expertise was clearly needed for production of the new gun. Elswick was chosen as the best place for the time being to manufacture this advanced weapon. The works on the Tyne possessed the know-how and the skills. Soon, the inventor was dividing his time supervising

A 12-pounder Armstrong gun and carriage.

production of his gun at Elswick and reorganising Woolwich.

However, how could this brilliant engineer serve as a senior government employee and also remain a partner in a company which was to receive armament orders from that government? To get around this problem it was decided that a new business concern would be formed, called the Elswick Ordnance Company, for the purpose of building the guns and that Armstrong should not play any part in this venture. The old company would continue to produce hydraulic machinery, with Armstrong remaining a partner in this separate concern.

Two men with great energy and ability joined the new ordnance company as managing partners. These were George Rendel, an engineer, and, a short time later, Andrew Noble, an expert in gun technology. Noble, an artillery captain and scientist with an extensive knowledge of ballistics who had been a government adviser, resigned his commission in the Army to join the new firm in 1860.

But the contract to produce guns for the British government was to be short-lived. Opposition within the Army and among rival arms manufacturers, particularly Joseph Whitworth of Manchester, led to a campaign against the Armstrong gun. Pressure was exerted on the government to return to muzzle-loading ordnance. The conservatism of Army officers, who regarded the new weapon as difficult to maintain and operate, was hard to overcome.

In late 1862 the government decided to cease ordering the gun from Elswick, only three years after officials had praised the weapon. The Army now had a large stock of the guns and Woolwich Arsenal, which Sir William had improved, was by this time able to meet supply requirements on its own. The government no longer needed arms from the North. In any case, muzzle-loading weapons were now back in favour. Indeed, it seems they had never been out of favour with a considerable number of senior officers. Many of the Armstrong guns were put into storage.

The inventor must have been disappointed by this setback to Tyneside, but he was not daunted. He resigned from his government posts the following year and returned to the Elswick Works. A lengthy wrangle with the government followed, but eventually a sum was agreed to compensate the Elswick Ordnance Company for its loss of business.

The orders for Britain had gone for the time being but at least the ordnance works was no longer tied to one customer. It was now on its own and free to pursue gun orders from foreign governments. The business turned its attention to naval guns. The Elswick Ordnance Company and W.G. Armstrong and Company were merged to form Sir W.G. Armstrong and

Company in 1864, with Sir William as chairman. The engineering and armaments sections were now united.

In 1866 one of George Rendel's brothers, Hamilton, joined the company and became a manager in the engineering department, alongside another man of great ability, Percy Westmacott. Meanwhile, a third Rendel brother, Stuart, acted as a salesman for Elswick , securing important foreign armament orders.

But ships as well as guns were destined to be built by Armstrong's company. In 1867 Sir William approached a leading shipbuilder on Tyneside, Charles Mitchell, of the Low Walker Yard in the East End of Newcastle. They agreed that Mitchell's yard would construct warships to be fitted with guns produced at Elswick.

The first ship to result from this joint venture was the gunboat *Staunch*, launched at the Low Walker Yard in 1868 for the British Admiralty. The ship and gun had been designed by George Rendel. Other gunboats followed, including several for Britain.

The removal of the 18th century bridge across the Tyne, which featured low, obstructive arches, and its replacement with the Swing Bridge in 1876 provided Sir William and his company with a gateway to the sea. They would now be able to open a shipyard at Elswick and export ships as well as guns along the watery highway of the Tyne.

In 1882 Charles Mitchell's shipbuilding business and Sir William's firm decided that their joint venture in building vessels should go a stage further. The two businesses were amalgamated to form Sir W.G. Armstrong, Mitchell and Co Ltd. In 1884 a shipyard was opened at Elswick and it was agreed that

A steam wherry, left, approaches the Swing Bridge on the Tyne. The High Level Bridge looms in the background. Armstrong's company built the superstructure and machinery for the Swing Bridge.

it would concentrate mainly on warship construction, while the Low Walker Yard would specialise in merchant vessels. The first vessel from the Elswick yard was the Austro-Hungarian torpedo cruiser *Panther*, launched in 1885.

Austria-Hungary was the first of many nations to place orders for warships at the new shipbuilding base. They included Britain, Japan, China, Argentina, Chile, Brazil, Norway, Portugal, Spain, Italy and Turkey. Elswick became particularly well known for its construction of cruisers, many of the early ones being designed by George Rendel. One of its most important customers was the Imperial Japanese Navy. Cruisers built at Elswick helped Admiral Togo of Japan to defeat a Russian fleet at the Battle of Tsushima in 1905. Many of Togo's guns in the battle had also been produced by the busy works on the Tyne.

In 1887 the battleship HMS *Victoria* was launched at the yard. This was an indication that Armstrong was by this time winning back the support of the British government for his products, although foreign orders remained for many years the most important element in the order books.

Elswick's business connections with Italy led the company to set up a gun-making factory and shipbuilding yard for the Italian government at Pozzuoli on the shores of the Bay of Naples. It began production in the late 1880s.

Meanwhile, on Tyneside, Armstrong's company continued to flourish. By 1895, when Armstrong himself was in semi-retirement, the Elswick Works was employing 11,000 people, mainly men and boys, and when the order book was full the workforce was sometimes increased to 13,000.

Also by 1895, the Elswick business featured a steel works as well as engineering and gun-making departments, the site having grown from five and a half acres to 50 acres. It stretched along the northern bank of the Tyne for nearly three quarters of a mile. Elswick had become an industrial empire with Armstrong as its emperor.

However, by this time the emperor was in his eighties and no longer involved in the everyday running of the business. He had created for himself a 'palace' in the Northumberland countryside.

*The battleship HMS **Victoria** passes down the Tyne on her delivery voyage to the Royal Navy in 1888. She had been built at Elswick.*

House Among The Crags

In 1826 Sir William's sister, Anne, had married William Henry Watson, a London lawyer who helped to train Armstrong in the legal profession. Anne gave birth to a son, John, in 1828 but only two months afterwards she died at the young age of 26.

Another blow occurred in 1851 when the man who had given the inventor such loyal support and friendship over the years, Armorer Donkin, passed away. True to his word, he left Sir William his money. It must have been something of a watershed in Sir William's life to lose this uncle figure who had encouraged his scientific, technical and business ventures. He and Anne shared fond memories of spending the summer and autumn holidays at Rothbury where they experienced Donkin's kindness.

And it was to Rothbury that Sir William's thoughts seemed to have continually returned. After his marriage to Margaret Ramshaw in 1835 he had a house built close to Jesmond Dene in Newcastle. He also later purchased much of the dene itself, a narrow valley of great beauty where he and his wife had many trees and shrubs planted. In addition, he commissioned the construction of the Banqueting Hall, a building on the western edge of the dene in which the industrialist entertained customers of the works. It was completed in 1862.

Sir William's house was known as Jesmond Dean (an unusual spelling of the more usual 'dene'), and being close to the centre of Newcastle it was clearly suitable during his days as a lawyer in the late 1830s and early 1840s. After the foundation of the Elswick Works in 1847, it was also suitable for the rising industrialist, the busy man of the world who needed to live within reasonable travelling distance of his factory.

But Sir William longed for a house in the country, a retreat which he could visit now and then in the summer to rest from the tensions of industry. His increasing wealth enabled him to fulfil this dream. He was able to create an imposing home in the magnificent countryside of Northumberland at Rothbury.

Many years later he was to say: 'When I resolved to have a country house I looked to Rothbury, because the district had many old associations for me. As a child I was often afflicted with a severe cough, and the physician used to order me to Rothbury where the air proved very beneficial.'

As a boy, the inventor had been familiar with a steep-sided, narrow valley a short distance from Rothbury through which the Debdon Burn flows to join the River Coquet. Its craggy sides still possess a rugged beauty which enthralls visitors.

Sir William chose this spot as the place where he would build a home, remote from the pressures of Elswick. The sides of the valley were said to be marred by dilapidated fences and broken down stone walls when he bought his first plot of land in the area in late 1863. The Elswick emperor was soon setting himself to work on directing the clearance of the fences and ruined walls and supervising the building of a house. This spacious but relatively modest home was perched on a ledge of rock well above the burn and with a craggy hillside towering above it. The work on its construction was begun in early 1864. The emperor named it Cragside.

A programme of planting trees and mosses was also started, again under the direction of the energetic Sir William, who seems to have been determined that the naked hillsides would be covered in a coat of magnificent and varied foliage. Here, as well as on the steep slopes of Jesmond Dene where trees had also been planted, the man whose career was linked so closely to machinery, guns and ships, showed his love of natural beauty by creating a green domain on the rocky Northumberland hillsides, which even today are adorned with a profusion of rhododendron flowers in spring and early summer.

Sir William added to the Cragside estate over the years by purchasing more land and directing the creation of lakes. Eventually seven million trees were planted in the grounds. By 1900 the estate featured 31 miles of carriage drives and walks.

As Sir William's wealth grew and the day-to-day running of Elswick was increasingly delegated to his trusted lieutenants, such as Andrew Noble, George Rendel and Percy Westmacott, the need to live near the great industrial base lessened. He was able to spend more time at Cragside. Indeed, it became his main home.

But the inventor was not content with his country house as originally built. In 1869 he commissioned one of the leading architects of the day, Richard Norman Shaw, to transform his home into a property fit for an industrial emperor and the following year the first plans were drawn up. Cragside was enlarged over a period of 15 years, during which time Norman Shaw undertook a programme of extensions. The result was that an imposing, romantic mansion took shape with a variation of interior styles. In this extraordinary house he was able

Cragside, c. 1890s. Lord Armstrong's home assumed the look of a fairytale baronial castle set amid the rugged Northumberland countryside. Guests were entertained in grand style. They included the Shah of Persia, and the prime minister of China.

to entertain guests and customers of Elswick in grand style.

The exterior of Cragside assumed the look of a fairy-tale baronial home set amid the rugged, tree-clad slopes of the hillside. The emperor's seat still looks impressively down upon the beautiful Debdon Burn, a testimony to wealth and power undoubtedly, but its surroundings are equally telling evidence of a man's love of nature.

The Benefactor

Sir William and Lady Armstrong had no children. Tensions may have existed in their marriage because of this, but if this was the case they were never publicly revealed. Sir William's great nephew, William Watson-Armstrong, the grandson of his sister Anne, became his heir.

In 1887, on the occasion of Queen Victoria's Jubilee, Sir William was created 1st Baron Armstrong of Cragside. The man who had often worked into the early hours of the morning during his pioneering days of establishing the Elswick Works was now a peer.

The childless but wealthy couple turned to charitable works, becoming benefactors of the North-East and in particular Newcastle. Lord Armstrong seems to have retained a strong affection for his native city and its people to the end of his life. It is certain that many people were helped by the couple's philanthropy. Some of the wealth generated by the workers and managers of Elswick was thus ploughed back into the community.

For example, Armstrong's attention had been drawn to the Northern Counties Institution for the Deaf and Dumb, a charitable school, when he learned that four apprentices at the Elswick Engine Works had been pupils there.

He also learned that the school had unsatisfactory premises in Charlotte Square, Newcastle. In 1859 the inventor was moved to make a contribution of £600 towards a fund which had been set up to build a new school for the deaf. His only

Armstrong College, Queen Victoria Road, Newcastle, c.1890. The Royal Victoria Infirmary was built opposite.

condition was that a similar sum should be raised by the end of the year to meet the target figure.

This move triggered a renewed effort and the sum needed was achieved. The new school was built on the edge of Newcastle's Town Moor. In 1893 he again gave money to the school, this time for it to be extended.

Armstrong also played a leading role in the foundation of the Fleming Memorial Hospital for Sick Children, the main building being situated on the edge of the Town Moor near the school for the deaf.

He provided the money for the hospital's new out-patient department in City Road, Newcastle. This building, opened in 1896, was a memorial to Lady Armstrong, who had died in 1893. It featured a dispensary and isolation rooms, which pro-vided temporary accommodation for children suffering from infectious diseases. William Cruddas, an MP and partner in

Armstrong's company, performed the opening ceremony, pointing out in his speech that the out-patient department would alleviate the sufferings of the many children whose parents were poor.

Lord Armstrong gave his money liberally to many other good causes. He and Lady Armstrong contributed a total of £11,500 towards the building of Newcastle's Hancock Natural History Museum, completed in 1878-82. This was an enormous sum in those days.

The emperor did not neglect his workforce. He promoted the education of apprentices by setting up a Literary and Mechanics Institute at Elswick where classes in various subjects were held. In addition, an Elswick elementary school and technical school were established.

He was also a benefactor of education outside the sphere of work. In 1871 he donated money towards the establishment of the city's College of Physical Science, which was set up two years later. It became known as Armstrong College in 1874, eventually amalgamating with the School of Medicine to become King's College, Durham University. It was a forerunner to the establishment of Newcastle University.

The baron of Cragside also gave considerable sums of money to the old Royal Infirmary in Newcastle, formerly known as Newcastle Infirmary. In the early 1870s he donated £2,700 for the building of a new operating theatre and in 1885 helped to finance the construction of an additional wing to the hospital known as the Ravensworth Wards with a gift of £1,000. He also gave £3,000 towards a fund set up to build a new hospital, which became the Royal Victoria Infirmary, opened in 1906.

The old mill in Jesmond Dene in 1887. Armstrong gave his lands at the dene to the people of Newcastle as a public park.

But perhaps Lord Armstrong's greatest gift to his beloved Newcastle was Jesmond Dene. In 1878 what seems to have been a surprise letter arrived at the council offices in the city. The benefactor announced his intention to give 26 acres of land on his Jesmond estate to the people of the city for their recreation and pleasure. This land, situated between Jesmond Dene and the present day Heaton Park, would become known as Armstrong Park.

Then, in 1883, he crowned this gift with another. This time he gave his land at Jesmond Dene to the people as a park. To this day it remains one of the city's most beautiful and distinctive spots. Few urban areas in Britain have a park to match it. Here, the waters of the Ouseburn flow through a steep-sided, narrow valley clad with trees and shrubs. Well within the city's boundaries, it provides a haven of peace.

A Down-to-Earth Man

Lord Armstrong was said to be courteous, unaffected and friendly in his manner, although quiet and retiring. He was modest and down-to-earth. The great engineer was not given to broad smiles or laughter, at least not in public, but nevertheless possessed a sense of humour, which displayed itself on occasions in his witty remarks.

The loud and enthusiastic welcome which the Prince and Princess of Wales received on their visit to Newcastle in 1884 prompted him to remark in a speech: 'I am sure that they (the royal couple) must be well satisfied with the manifestations of loyalty which they have seen this day, and dispense with a repetition of them on the occasion of their second visit.' The joke prompted loud laughter.

He comes across to us as a man of few words and calm bearing but of undoubted wit, humanity and courtesy. These qualities, combined with his generosity to the community, may explain why he was so well respected and held in affection by many people in the North-East.

In old age Armstrong frequently talked of his mother, Ann. He paid for the building of 12 fine almshouses at the eastern end of Rothbury village in memory of her. A tablet on one of the homes reads: 'Erected by William George Baron Armstrong of Cragside in memory of Ann Armstrong his much loved mother, 1896.'

The *World* magazine declared in 1879 that Armstrong was 'a Newcastle lad in his speech, he is also a genuine Tynesider

The elderly baron. Lord Armstrong at Cragside in the 1890s. His semi-retirement was an extremely active one. He carried out research into electricity in a laboratory at the house.

in his quiet force of character ... yet to judge from the outside, from simple sight and sound, he is the mildest mannered and most gentle of Northumbria's sons'.

On fishing expeditions as a boy he was not averse to a little poaching on the River Coquet. He would go out alone on such trips to catch a few 'unofficial' fish. It was said many years later that this was why Armstrong, when serving as chairman of the Rothbury Bench of magistrates, dealt leniently with poachers who were brought before him.

Courteous in his remarks to his fellow men, he expected courtesy returned. Like Sir Joseph Porter in Gilbert and Sullivan's operetta *HMS Pinafore*, he strongly disliked swearing of any kind, which he described as a 'vulgar practice'. A story was told that in Armstrong's early days at Cragside, when Elswick guns were tested on the hill above the house, a young man, a student at the works, was helping to test a gun. Something went wrong, and the student exclaimed 'Oh damn the thing.' But he suddenly realised that Armstrong had heard him and he immediately apologised. Accepting the apology, Armstrong replied: 'If swearing will advance science, swear away as long as you like. But if it won't, what is the good of it?'

Lord Armstrong's kindness towards children was another element in his character. For example, in the winter of 1891-92, when Armstrong was in his 80s, he was walking through the snow to one of the lakes at Cragside where guests and Rothbury villagers were skating. Some small boys were sliding close to the edge of the ice, but when they saw him standing nearby they were a little in awe of him and stopped playing. Armstrong noticed this and said: 'Go on with your sliding my boys, don't let me stop you.' But the suggestion seemed to increase their shyness. Armstrong decided to put them at their ease and he began sliding like a boy himself, inviting them to join him. He said: 'Come along boys. We'll soon have a grand slide.' The boys accepted the invitation and soon there were smiles all round.

In January 1889 he stood for election to Northumberland County Council. His opponent, who lost, was a Robert Donkin, of Haw Hill, Rothbury. The lord of Cragside showed his generosity and humour when he sent two pheasants to Donkin as a Christmas gift. Armstrong wrote: 'Cragside, December 24, 1888. Dear Sir – We are foes till after the election, but the game won't keep till then. I think it better to send it now.' Armstrong served on the county council from 1889 to 1892. In politics, he was a right-wing Liberal, being strongly opposed to Home Rule for Ireland. He stood in Newcastle as a Liberal Unionist candidate for Parliament in the general election of 1886. The Home Rule issue dominated the campaign. However, the emperor was defeated.

Armstrong, in common with many other employers, resisted trade unions. His company opposed calls for shorter working hours. He fought against the engineers' struggle for a nine-hour day in 1871 but was ultimately forced to concede it. However, in 1897 the engineering workers at Elswick were locked out when they sought an eight-hour day in another struggle with their employer. The company maintained its stance, cracks appeared in the engineers' unity and after many months of hardship the men returned to work without achieving their objective.

Northern Lights

In August 1884 Armstrong had the honour of receiving the Prince and Princess of Wales as guests at Cragside. The royal couple and their children stayed for three nights.

They arrived at Rothbury by train on August 19 and in the evening the grounds of the Cragside estate were illuminated with thousands of lights to mark their visit.

Ten thousand glass lamps were hung amid the rocky slopes and on the railings lining the walks. In addition, vast numbers of Chinese lanterns were strung between the trees. The illuminations took the estate's workmen two hours to light.

To complete this extraordinary spectacle six large balloons were sent up from the grounds carrying powerful magnesium lights of changeable colours and fireworks. The royal couple were also able to look out from the house and see a huge bonfire blazing on Simonside hill.

But it was the lights inside Armstrong's great home which were the most extraordinary and which the prince and princess must have marvelled at most of all. Pioneering experiments in lighting a house by electricity had been carried out there.

In 1878 Armstrong made his residence the first home in the world to be lit by hydro-electricity. Water was harnessed for this purpose by erecting a dam on one of the lakes above the house. This was linked up with a turbine which powered a Siemens dynamo. The electricity provided the light for an arc lamp which illuminated the picture gallery in the house.

Two years later more than 40 incandescent filament lamps, invented by the famous Newcastle scientist Joseph Swan who was a friend of Armstrong, were set up in the mansion among the crags, this time including the library as well as the gallery. Armstrong went on to improve on his first water power arrangements by having a small hydro-electricity 'station' built in the grounds, using water from other lakes on the estate.

Joseph Swan recalled: 'So far as I know Cragside was the first house in England to be fitted with my electric lamps. I had greatly wished that it should be, and when I told Lord Armstrong he readily assented.

Prince Albert Edward and Princess Alexandra, who visited Newcastle and Cragside in 1884.

'There had, previously to the introduction of the incandescent lamp into the house, been an arc lamp in the picture gallery. That was taken down and my lamps substituted. It was a delightful experience for both of us when the gallery was first lit up.

'The speed of the dynamo had not been quite rightly adjusted to produce the strength of current in the lamps that they required. The speed was too fast and the current too strong. Consequently, the lamps were above their normal brightness, but the effect was splendid and never to be forgotten.'

On August 20 the Prince and Princess of Wales journeyed from Rothbury by train to Newcastle where they received a tumultuous welcome. As the royal couple emerged from the Central Station to board their carriage, drawn by four bay horses, they were greeted by a crowd waving thousands of handkerchiefs and hats.

A procession of carriages, headed by the one carrying the royal couple and their children, then wended its way through Newcastle's streets to deafening cheers from the huge crowds. Men of the Northumberland Hussars formed an escort for the royal party.

Buildings along the line of the route featured elaborate decorations. In Collingwood Street and Mosley Street arches of evergreens had been put up. In Grey Street a temporary triumphal arch in Corinthian style had been erected at a cost of £200. Indeed, the lavish spending on the decorations was reported to have been strongly criticised by 'radicals'.

Sir William, as he then was, and Lady Armstrong, together with his nephew John Watson and his wife, journeyed in one

*Benton Bridge, now known as Armstrong Bridge, over Jesmond Dene. From the **Record of the Royal Visit of 1884**.*

of the carriages along the streets. Elswick's emperor seems to have been cheered by the crowds almost as much as the prince.

The carriages drove by way of Byker Bridge to Heaton and then crossed the New Benton Bridge spanning the valley of the Ouseburn, built by Armstrong's firm and later named Armstrong Bridge. The carriages then headed for the Banqueting Hall at Jesmond Dene. The emperor of the North had by this time given the hall to the city as well as the dene.

The Mayor of Newcastle Dr Henry Newton told the prince in a speech that the dene was 'the gift of a distinguished citizen and will associate for all time the honoured name of Armstrong with our public benefactors'.

The prince, later to become Edward VII, then officially

declared the dene open as a public park and was presented with a golden key as a memento of the occasion. Afterwards, the princess planted a turkey oak on the grassy slopes close to the hall.

On the same day the prince also officially opened Newcastle's Hancock Natural History Museum near Barras Bridge and the reference department of the Public Library in New Bridge Street. Another triumphal arch had been put up in Barras Bridge close to St Thomas's Church and it bore the inscription 'Welcome to Canny Newcastle.'

A civic lunch was held at St George's Hall attended by many leading dignitaries. Armstrong was among those who gave speeches. He told the prince: 'An inspection of our places of industry which omits a view of the Elswick Works is rather like the play of Hamlet with the part of the prince left out.' He added that he knew it was impossible for the busy royal guest to see Elswick on this occasion but he hoped he would do so on a return visit.

Later, the royal party journeyed back to Rothbury by train and stayed a second night at Cragside. That evening a spectacular fireworks display complete with rockets and a bonfire was held at Cow Hill on Newcastle's Town Moor. Hotels, shops and other buildings in the city centre featured decorative lights to mark the occasion.

The following day the royal couple returned to Newcastle and boarded the paddle steamer *Para-e-Amazonas* at the Quayside. The vessel then sailed down the Tyne, enabling the prince to gain a view of the various shipyards along its banks.

Just before passing Andrew Leslie's Hebburn Shipyard, which had built the *Para-e-Amazonas*, the royal visitors were

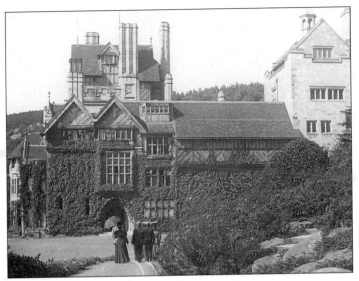

Cragside c.1900.

greeted by 3,000 schoolchildren from Hebburn and surrounding areas who stood on the town's Ballast Hills by the riverbank and formed a huge shape resembling the design of the Prince of Wales's feathers.

On reaching North Shields, the steamer headed for the newly completed dock at Coble Dene which the prince officially opened when the *Para-e-Amazonas* broke a double line of blue ribbon stretched across the narrow entrance. It was officially named the Albert Edward Dock in his honour.

The royal party later continued their journey to Tynemouth and then returned once more to Cragside for a third night as Armstrong's guests. In the morning they departed for Edinburgh by train. Their host was no doubt delighted with the success of the visit.

To Rothbury Church

Margaret, Lady Armstrong, died in 1893 at the age of 86, leaving her husband a widower at the great house above the Debdon Burn. However, he was not a lonely widower. Armstrong received regular visits from his nephew John, great nephew William and their wives. He lived long enough to see his great nephew's two small children during his final years.

His great nephew adopted the surname Armstrong, becoming William Watson-Armstrong and towards the end of the emperor's life became his secretary, spending long periods living at the house. In addition, many important foreign guests were entertained at Cragside from time to time.

Although remaining chairman, in his last 30 or so years Lord Armstrong played a far less active role in the affairs of his company, leaving Andrew Noble to increasingly take control of the day-to-day running

Margaret, Lady Armstrong, who died at Jesmond Dene in 1893.

of the business. Instead, he concentrated on continuing to develop the Cragside estate, the planting of trees and shrubs being one of his passions, and also carried out scientific research in a laboratory at the house.

As a young man, Armstrong had invented a machine which produced electricity by means of high-pressure steam. As a result, he had been made a Fellow of the Royal Society. Now, in semi-retirement, he returned to electricity as his main subject of research.

His semi-retirement was an extremely active one and he remained energetic throughout his 70s and 80s. Displaying an undimmed love of science and the quest for knowledge, he spent long hours in his Cragside laboratory during 1894-96.

Bamburgh Castle around 1890. Armstrong bought it in 1894.

This work proved fruitful, for in 1897 he published a book, *Electrical Movement in Air and Water*. It contained photographs taken by his friend and assistant, John Worsnop.

Despite this absorption in scientific work, Armstrong still sometimes turned his thoughts to charitable deeds. In 1894, he bought Bamburgh Castle on the north Northumberland coast and started a project to turn it into a convalescent home.

He also found time to entertain visiting foreign rulers and dignitaries at his house. They were taken on tours of the Elswick Works, which had now spread along the banks of the Tyne to Scotswood. These visits helped to win orders for his company. In 1889 the Shah of Persia came to Cragside. In 1896 the prime minister of China, Li Hung Chang, also stayed there, and a year later the King of Siam was a guest at the impressive mansion.

Lord Armstrong died at Cragside at 1.10am on December 27 1900. He was aged 90. He was reported to have passed away peacefully. His great nephew William Watson-Armstrong inherited his fortune. In his memory, Watson-Armstrong gave £100,000 towards the fund for the building of the new Royal Victoria Infirmary in Newcastle. It was a third of the cost of constructing and equipping the hospital, which was opened by Edward VII in 1906. Money created by the production of guns and warships capable of destroying life was thus by an extreme irony used to save lives and relieve suffering.

Armstrong's partner, Andrew Noble, who by this time had also received a knighthood, succeeded him as chairman of the company, which in 1897 had merged with Whitworth of Manchester to become Sir W.G. Armstrong Whitworth & Co Ltd.

*The Argentinian cruiser **9 de Julio**, built at Elswick, steams under the High Level Bridge on the Tyne in 1893.*

Workmen polish guns at Elswick. The Works became one of the largest arsenals in the world.

By 1900 the Elswick Works were truly the hub of an industrial empire employing many thousands of people. At Elswick guns were produced ranging in size from great 110-ton breech-loaders to small machine-guns, manufactured under licence from the Gatling company.

The works also featured shops in which huge steel mountings were made to carry giant armour-piercing guns as well as tiny carriages for small seven-pounder guns capable of being carried by mules into mountain terrain. Also by 1900, the engineering department had played a role in building major bridges as well as cranes and other machinery. For example, it constructed the opening machinery for London's Tower Bridge. In addition, the Elswick Yard had become a world-renowned builder of warships. Its cruisers were a noted speciality. The Low Walker Yard was equally famous for its pioneering oil tankers, ice breakers and other merchant vessels.

The company went on to make an immense contribution to Britain's efforts during the First World War when it manufactured 13,000 guns, over 14 million shells and around 100 tanks. Warships continued to be launched for Britain's fleet, a considerable number fighting at the Battle of Jutland in 1916. The firm expanded into aircraft production, setting up a biplane factory on the edge of Newcastle's Town Moor to supply Britain's emerging airforce.

After the war, the Elswick output included locomotives. In 1927-28 many of the company's business interests were merged with those of Vickers to form Vickers-Armstrongs Ltd. The Elswick Works continued in production and contributed to Britain's efforts during the Second World War, again manufacturing guns and tanks. The company's Walker Naval Yard in the East End of Newcastle launched and repaired many warships during the conflict. It had replaced the shipyard at Elswick.

Lord Armstrong's funeral on December 31 1900 had a dignified simplicity. There were no fine horses with plumes, nor was there an elaborate hearse or military guard of honour. Instead, the great engineer's body was borne to Rothbury Parish Church on a rolley, a simple farm cart, drawn by ordinary working horses. The rolley was draped in a purple cloth.

The coffin, made of oak with brass mountings, was carried from Cragside house to the rolley by workmen and tenants of the estate. After them, came Lord Armstrong's valet, Andrew Crosier, and the butler, Mr T. Mitchell.

Among those in the 12 carriages following the rolley as it

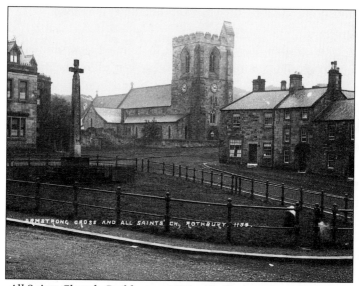

All Saints Church, Rothbury, c.1910 with the Armstrong Cross in the foreground. The cross was erected in 1902 as a memorial to Lord and Lady Armstrong. It stands on the site of Rothbury's ancient market cross.

proceeded towards the Rothbury road on that damp day were Mr and Mrs Watson-Armstrong, Sir Andrew Noble, Percy Westmacott and the Duke of Northumberland. The shops in Rothbury were closed. The Cragside estate provided employment for many of the villagers.

Even in death, Armstrong's foreign connections were evident. Wreaths were received from a retired rear admiral in the Argentinian navy and from Japanese overseers who had been working at Elswick. The funeral service included the hymn *Now the Labourer's Task is O'er*. The emperor had indeed worked tirelessly throughout his long life.

Lord Armstrong was buried in Rothbury Churchyard beside his wife Margaret. He lies in a quiet corner close to the meandering River Coquet which was so dear to his heart.

The ships, guns and steel have gone, along with the Elswick Works. The instruments of war hold no affection in people's hearts. But each spring and early summer the rhododendrons of Cragside burst into bloom and the trees of Jesmond Dene wear a mantle of fresh foliage to be enjoyed by people of all ages and incomes. These two places of rare beauty are Lord Armstrong's legacy to posterity. They remain his most charming memorials.

LORD ARMSTRONG'S HEIR

In 1903 Lord Armstrong's great nephew and heir, William Watson-Armstrong (1863-1941), received a peerage, becoming the 1st Baron Armstrong of the second creation. Bamburgh now joined Cragside in the baronial title.

Bibliography and further reading:

Newcastle Daily Chronicle.

Newcastle Daily Journal.

The Ludgate Monthly.

Baron Armstrong of Cragside. A collection of items relating to Lord Armstrong. (In Newcastle City Libraries' Local Studies Collection).

The Royal Visit 1884. Record of the visit of their Royal Highnesses the Prince and Princess of Wales to Newcastle upon Tyne and Tyneside. (Andrew Reid, Newcastle, 1885).

Cragside. (The National Trust, 1981. Reprinted with amendments 1983, 1984.)

The Great Gun Maker. The Life of Lord Armstrong. By David Dougan. (Frank Graham, 1970).

The Making of the Tyne. By R.W. Johnson. (Walter Scott, 1895).

Down Elswick Slipways. Armstrong's Ships and People 1884-1918. By Dick Keys and Ken Smith. (Newcastle City Libraries, 1996).

W.G. Armstrong. The Life & Times of Sir William Armstrong, Baron Armstrong of Cragside. By Peter McKenzie. (Longhirst Press, Newcastle, 1983).

Armstrongs of Elswick. By Kenneth Warren. (The Macmillan Press, 1989.)